Audit Report

Report Number: OIG-SBLF-12-003

STATE SMALL BUSINESS CREDIT INITIATIVE: California Needs to Improve Its Oversight of Programs Participating in the State Small Business Credit Initiative

May 24, 2012

Office of Inspector General

Department of the Treasury

Contents

Audit Report

Results in Brief 2

Background 4

California Generally Used SSBCI Funds Properly, but Misused $133,250 in Loan Loss Reserves Supporting Three Loan Guarantees 6

California Did Not Comply with Program Requirements for Borrower and Lender Assurances 10

Recommendations 13

Appendices

Appendix 1: Objectives, Scope, and Methodology 17
Appendix 2: Management Response 20
Appendix 3: Report Distribution 38

Abbreviations

BTHA	California Business, Transportation, and Housing Agency
CalCAP	California Capital Access Program
CPCFA	California Pollution Control Financing Authority
FDC	Financial Development Corporation
OIG	Office of Inspector General
OMB	Office of Management and Budget
SBLGP	California Small Business Loan Guarantee Program
SSBCI	State Small Business Credit Initiative
The Act	The Small Business Jobs Act of 2010

OIG

Audit Report

The Department of the Treasury
Office of Inspector General

May 24, 2012

Don Graves, Jr.
Deputy Assistant Secretary for Small Business, Housing, and Community Development

This report presents the results of our audit of the state of California's use of funds awarded under the State Small Business Credit Initiative (SSBCI), which was established by the Small Business Jobs Act of 2010 (the Act). California was awarded $168.6 million, and in February 2011 received $55.6 million of the awarded funds. The State has divided these funds equally between two existing small business development programs—the California Capital Access Program (CalCAP) and the California Small Business Loan Guarantee Program (SBLGP). At the time of our audit in October 2011, the State had obligated or spent approximately $3.6 million of the first tranche.

The Act requires the Treasury Office of Inspector General (OIG) to conduct audits of the use of funds made available under SSBCI and to identify any instances of reckless or intentional misuse. Treasury has defined reckless misuse as a use of funds that the participating state or administering entity should have known was unauthorized or prohibited, and which is a highly unreasonable departure or willful disregard from the standards of ordinary care. Intentional misuse is any unauthorized or prohibited use of funds that the participating state or its administering entity knew was unauthorized or prohibited.

Our audit objectives were to: (1) test participant compliance with program requirements and prohibitions to identify reckless or intentional misuse; and (2) evaluate California's oversight of CalCAP and SBLGP in order to assess the risk of waste, fraud, abuse, and non-compliance with the requirements of the Act. We also followed up on recommendations from our August 5, 2011 report[1] that Treasury (1)

---

[1] OIG-SBLF-11-002, STATE SMALL BUSINESS CREDIT INITIATIVE: Treasury Needs to Strengthen State Accountability for Use of Funds, August 5, 2011.

require each state to make a representation that it is aware of, monitoring and enforcing compliance with Treasury's policy guidelines and restrictions, and (2) require that the designated state agency responsible for administering SSBCI funds collect and review borrower and lender compliance assurances.

To test participant compliance, we reviewed a judgmental sample of 73 small business loans enrolled in the two state programs as of September 30, 2011. We reviewed the loans to determine whether they complied with program requirements for loan use, capital at risk, and other restrictions. We also reviewed the administrative costs both programs charged against SSBCI funds to ensure they were accurate and supported in accordance with Treasury Guidelines and Office of Management and Budget (OMB) Circular A-87, *Cost Principles for State, Local, and Indian Tribal Government*.[2] To evaluate the State of California's oversight of CalCAP and SBLGP, we reviewed the State's compliance programs, and interviewed management and staff from the designated administering entities—the California Pollution Control Financing Authority (CPCFA) and the California Business, Transportation, and Housing Agency (BTHA), respectively. We also visited 6 of the 11 Financial Development Corporations (FDCs) that were given program responsibility for SBLGP and 3 lenders participating in CalCAP. Appendix 1 contains a more detailed description of our audit objectives, scope, and methodology.

We conducted our audit between October 2011 and March 2012 in accordance with Government Auditing Standards. Those standards require that we plan and perform the audit to obtain sufficient, appropriate evidence to provide a reasonable basis for our findings and conclusions based on our audit objectives. We believe that the evidence obtained to address our audit objectives provides a reasonable basis for our findings and conclusions.

Results In Brief

Based on our sample results, we determined that the majority of the $3.6 million expended by the state of California was used properly.

---

[2] Office of Management and Budget Circular Number A-87, revised May 10, 2004.

However, we identified $133,250 in loan loss reserves funded under SBLGP that did not comply with SSBCI program requirements. These non-compliant expenditures constitute a "reckless" misuse of funds as defined by Treasury guidance, which under the provisions of the Small Business Jobs Act must be recouped. The State also did not properly report $160,988 in administrative expenses charged to the SSBCI program. These expenses were reasonable, but not allowable or allocable because they were not adequately supported by actual expenses incurred or with proper documentation to validate the costs claimed. Therefore, the entire amount is considered questioned costs.

Additionally, 42 or approximately 58 percent, of the 73 loans we tested lacked all of the required borrower and lender assurances. Of this amount, there were 31 CalCAP loans that were missing borrower assurances and 11 SBLGP loans that were missing borrower and/or lender assurances. One loan also went to a borrower that had the same residence as a registered sex offender. The State was unaware of these issues and did not collect borrower and lender assurances because Treasury did not require it to do so. In August 2011, we recommended that designated state entities responsible for administering SSBCI funds be required to collect and review such assurances, and that each state be required to make a representation that it is aware of, monitoring, and enforcing compliance with program requirements.

Treasury agreed to address the collection of lender and borrower assurances, but asserted that representations were unnecessary because assurances submitted with quarterly reports already mandated under Section 4.7 of the Allocation Agreement would serve that purpose. For September and December 2011, California provided Treasury with quarterly reports affirming that it had complied with program requirements. However, we found a non-compliance rate of 58 percent for the loans reviewed in our sample. This non-compliance rate renders California's reports materially inaccurate, and accordingly we believe there has been a general event of default under California's Allocation Agreement. Treasury, therefore, needs to consider whether future disbursements to California should be suspended or terminated.

We recommend that Treasury recoup from California the $133,250 we identified as a "reckless" misuse of funds, disallow the $160,988 in administrative expenses unless California can demonstrate that it was based on actual costs, and consider what additional action, if any, should be taken, including potentially withholding future funding for administrative expenses until reporting practices have been corrected. Further, we are recommending that Treasury determine whether there has been a general event of default under the Allocation Agreement, and determine whether the event warrants suspension or termination of future funding to California. Finally, we recommend that Treasury require California to report back on its compliance with the borrower and lender assurance requirements, and the sex offender status of one borrower.

On May 11, 2012, Treasury submitted a formal response, agreeing to take the recommended actions as part of its broader compliance management process. Management's response, which includes a letter from California that articulates the actions California is taking to address the report's concerns, is contained in its entirety in Appendix 2 to this report. The corrective actions, if implemented as described, meet the intent of the recommendations.

Background

SSBCI is a $1.5 billion Treasury program that provides participating states, territories and eligible municipalities with funding to strengthen Capital Access Programs and other credit support programs that provide financial assistance to small businesses and manufacturers. Capital Access Programs provide portfolio insurance for business loans based on a separate loan loss reserve fund for each participating financial institution. Other credit support programs include collateral support, loan participation, loan guarantee, and venture capital programs. Each participating state is required to designate specific departments, agencies, or political subdivisions to implement the programs approved for funding. The designated state entity distributes the SSBCI funds to various public and private institutions, which may include a subdivision of another state, a for-profit entity supervised by the state, or a non-profit entity supervised by the state. These entities use funds to make loans or provide credit access to small businesses.

Primary oversight of the use of SSBCI funds is the responsibility of each participant. To ensure that funds are properly controlled and expended, the Act requires that Treasury execute an Allocation Agreement with participants setting forth internal controls, and compliance and reporting requirements before allocating SSBCI funds. SSBCI disbursements to participating states are made in three tranches: the first when the Secretary approves the state for participation; and the second and third after the participating state certifies that it has obligated, transferred or spent at least 80 percent of the previous tranche. In addition, the participating state is required to certify that it has complied with all applicable program requirements.

On August 5, 2011, we identified several areas where Treasury's compliance and oversight framework for SSBCI could be improved. Among other recommendations, we noted that the Allocation Agreement should clearly define the oversight obligations of participating states, and that each state should be required to make a representation that it is aware of, monitoring, and enforcing compliance with Treasury's policy guidelines and restrictions. Further, we recommended that Treasury require each designated state agency that is responsible for administering SSBCI funds to collect and review compliance assurances made by lenders and borrowers.

The State of California's Participation in the SSBCI

On February 17, 2011, Treasury approved California's separate applications for CalCAP and SBLGP, awarding each approximately $84.3 million for a total of $168.6 million. That same month Treasury disbursed the first tranche of the state's allocation, $55.6 million. At the time of our audit in October 2011, California had obligated or spent approximately $3.6 million of the first tranche. Of the $3.6 million, $171,007 had been used to pay administrative costs associated with implementing the two programs.

SBLGP, administered by BTHA, was started in 1971 and provides guarantees for loans issued to small businesses by private institutions, typically banks. The loan guarantees cover a percentage of the loan balance and interest in the event of default, thereby offsetting some losses a financial institution may incur from loan defaults. BTHA has designated 11 FDCs located throughout California to: (1) market the SBLGP program; (2) coordinate the packaging of loan guarantee applications between small businesses and financial institutions; and (3) issue the loan guarantees. As of September 30, 2011, BTHA had used approximately $2.47 million of SSBCI funds to guarantee 55 loans totaling approximately $9.9 million in value.

CalCAP, administered by CPCFA, provides portfolio insurance to lenders that is financed by insurance premiums paid by the borrowers and lenders for each loan enrolled. The premiums, which are deposited in a lender's loan loss reserve fund, range between 2 to 3.5 percent of the loan enrollment amount. CalCAP contributes an amount that is at least equal to the sum of the borrower and lender contributions. As of September 30, 2011, CPCFA had enrolled 449 loans totaling approximately $22 million in its SSBCI program. The total Federal contribution to lender loan loss reserve funds associated with these loans was approximately $950,000.

California Generally Used SSBCI Funds Properly, but Misused $133,250 in Loan Loss Reserves Supporting Three Loan Guarantees

Of the 73 loans sampled, 70 or approximately 96 percent, complied with the requirements established for the SSBCI program. However, we identified $133,250 in misuse associated with loan loss reserves for three SBLGP loan guarantees that were not compliant. All of these instances met the definition of "reckless" misuse, requiring Treasury to recoup the misused funds.

Additionally, we found that $160,988 incurred for administering SSBCI funds was not properly supported as required by OMB Circular A-87. Of this amount, $153,777 was charged against the SBLGP program by BTHA. Instead of basing administrative expenses on incurred costs, BTHA estimated the administrative expenses associated with administering SBLGP. BTHA also lacked proper documentation to validate the costs claimed. The remaining $7,211 was associated with personnel expenses under CalCAP that were not properly documented.

Funds Associated with Three Loan Guarantees Were Misused

The Act provides that SSBCI funds cannot be used to fund business activities that Treasury has prohibited for enrollment in the program and requires that lenders have a meaningful amount of their own capital at risk in loans enrolled with SSBCI funds. To implement these provisions, Treasury issued guidance in December 2010 prohibiting loans guaranteed with SSBCI funds from being used for partial changes of business ownership or changes that will not benefit the business. The guidance also required lenders to bear 10 percent or more of the loss from a loan default, and limits the state guarantee to no more than 90 percent.[3] In April 2011, Treasury raised the minimum lender loss burden to 20 percent and reduced the state guarantee limit to 80 percent.

Although loans we reviewed generally complied with Treasury's requirements, we identified three that did not. As described below, one loan guarantee did not comply with the loan purpose prohibitions and two did not comply with the capital-at-risk thresholds:

- One FDC issued a $25,000 guarantee, of which $15,000 was used to pay off the balance of a debt due to the former owner of a business. A representative from the FDC stated that it was unaware that using the loan proceeds to purchase a portion of an ownership interest in a business was prohibited. BTHA provided $6,250 (25 percent of the total guarantee) in SSBCI funds to the bank's loan loss reserve fund in support of the guarantee.

- Another FDC issued two 90-percent guarantees totaling $518,000, exceeding the 80-percent guarantee limit set by Treasury. BTHA provided $129,500 (25 percent of the total guarantee) in SSBCI funds to the loan loss reserve fund in support of the guarantees. Both guarantees were issued after Treasury established the 80-percent guaranty limit and 20-

---

[3] This guidance also lists other prohibitions.

percent-lender-capital-at-risk requirements. State officials told us they contacted Treasury to determine which guarantee threshold applied because loans had been negotiated before the April guidelines were issued. However, Treasury officials told us they had requested additional documentation from the State to render a decision, but the State did not provide the information. As a result, Treasury did not approve the State's use of the higher guarantee level. However, the State issued the guarantees without further guidance from Treasury.

All three noncompliant loan guarantees met Treasury's definition of "reckless" misuse of funds, which would require the State to refund to Treasury the portion of its allocation associated with the misuse. A "reckless" misuse of funds is a use that the participating state or administering entities should have known was unauthorized or prohibited, and which is a highly unreasonable departure or willful disregard from the standards of ordinary care.

By signing the Allocation Agreement, the State acknowledged that it and the entities designated to administer the funds for the State were aware of the program requirements prescribed by Treasury and would comply with them. With respect to the first loan, the FDC that approved the guarantee should have known that the loan use was prohibited. The FDC had received Treasury's December 2010 guidance outlining the types of uses that were prohibited, and reviewed the guarantee form, which disclosed the purpose of the loan. However, the FDC did not check the guidance when enrolling the loan or establish a process for determining whether the loans it enrolled were consistent with Treasury guidance. For the second two loans, the originating FDC knew the loan guarantee limits it approved exceeded the authorized level because it had received Treasury's April guidelines, which reduced the maximum guarantee level to 80 percent. The FDC also discussed this issue with State officials, who acknowledged that the loan guarantees exceeded program restrictions when it contacted Treasury to request an exception to the guidance. The State nonetheless issued the guarantees at the 90-percent level without receiving Treasury's approval.

We find that the State and its administering entities should have known that the intended use of funds in all three instances was unauthorized or prohibited. For the first loan, we believe that failure to check the guidelines or to create a process to determine whether a loan purpose conforms with the guidelines prior to enrollment is highly unreasonable. With respect to the second two loans, the State discussed the excessive guarantees with Treasury, but did not secure its approval before proceeding. Therefore, the guarantee levels awarded also demonstrated a highly unreasonable departure from or willful disregard of the standards of ordinary care. Because the Act requires recoupment of funds identified by OIG as intentionally or recklessly misused, Treasury will need to recover the $133,250 in misused funds associated with the financing of loan loss reserves for the three loan guarantees.

Administrative Costs for SBLGP and CalCAP Were Not Allowable or Allocable

We also found that BTHA and CPCFA did not fully account for $160,988 in administrative expenses charged to the SSBCI program. As of September 30, 2011, BTHA had reported SBLGP administrative expenses of $153,777, representing 4.3 percent of the $3.6 million used from the first SSBCI tranche. CalCAP had reported $17,230 in administrative expenses for the same time period, representing approximately 0.5 percent of the $3.6 million used from the first SSBCI tranche. Participating states may charge up to 5 percent of their first SSBCI tranche for expenses associated with implementing the program, and must follow cost standards for state and local governments as prescribed in OMB Circular A-87.

According to the OMB circular, only actual expenses incurred that are allowable, reasonable, and allocable can be considered chargeable costs. We determined that the entire $153,777 charged for SBLGP administrative expenses and $7,211 of the $17,230 charged for CalCAP administrative expenses were reasonable, but not allowable or allocable because they were not adequately supported by actual expenses incurred or with the proper documentation to validate the costs claimed. The SBLGP expenses claimed were based on budget estimates made by SBLGP officials. In discussing the questioned costs with BTHA officials, they acknowledged that they had not followed Federal requirements in charging administrative costs to the SSBCI program. We also questioned $7,211 in personnel expenses claimed by CalCAP for which it was not able to provide adequate documentation.

Because BTHA and CPCFA are not accounting for all administrative costs correctly, Treasury should disallow the $160,988 unless BTHA and CPCFA can provide supporting documentation. Treasury should also withhold the administrative portion of future tranches until BTHA and CalCAP have corrected their reporting practices.

California Did Not Comply with Program Requirements for Borrower and Lender Assurances

The Act and Treasury guidelines require that lenders obtain borrower assurances that (1) loan proceeds will be used for approved business purposes, (2) the borrower is eligible to receive SSBCI funding, and (3) the principals of the borrower have not been convicted of a sex offense against a minor. Additionally, under Treasury's guidelines, each state must obtain an assurance from the financial institution lender affirming that:

- The loan is not for prior debt that is not covered under the approved state program or that was owed to the lender or an affiliate of the lender;

- The loan is not a refinancing of a loan previously made to the borrower by the lender or an affiliate of the lender; and

- No principal of the lender has been convicted of a sex offense against a minor.[4]

---

[4] Under Treasury's April 2011 guidelines, "principal" is defined as: the proprietor of a sole proprietorship; each partner in a partnership; each of the five most highly compensated executives, officers, or employees of a corporation, limited liability company, association or a development company; or each direct or indirect holder of 20 percent or more of the ownership stock or stock equivalent of that entity.

Despite these requirements, 42, or approximately 58 percent, of the 73 loans we tested lacked all of the required borrower and/or lender assurances. Of this amount, 31 CalCAP loans were missing borrower assurances and 11 SBLGP loans were missing borrower and/or lender assurances.

Of the 41 loans missing borrower assurances, 28 were missing 2 of the assurances and 13 were missing all 3 assurances. We also determined that a registered sex offender had the same residence as one of the borrowers who had not provided an assurance as to his sex offender status. To ensure that the borrower is not a sex offender or has not obtained a loan to benefit a sex offender, Treasury will need to ensure that the State further investigates the sex offender status of the borrower and that loan proceeds are being used for an eligible purpose.

We discussed the missing borrower assurances with CPCFA and BTHA officials that administer CalCAP and SBLGP, respectively. CPCFA officials told us they are currently preparing a lender instruction letter providing guidelines and deadlines for lenders to obtain missing borrower assurances on existing loans. In addition, CPCFA officials told us they are implementing a schedule for lender site visits and desk audits, and anticipate that the first site visit will commence in March 2012. BTHA officials reported that they have collected 9 of the 10 missing borrower assurances identified by the audit. Treasury will need to follow up with CPCFA and BTHA to ensure that all of the missing assurances are collected.

The State was unaware of the missing borrower and lender assurances because it had not collected them from lenders as it was not required to do so by Treasury. Treasury relies on participating states to submit quarterly certifications that its SSBCI-funded programs are being implemented in accordance with requirements of the Act and Treasury guidelines. However, our audit demonstrated that although California provided those certifications in September and December 2011, the State programs were not being implemented in accordance with all program requirements because the assurances had not been obtained. Moreover, the results show that the State did not collect the information needed to support its certifications to Treasury that its use of funds compiled with program requirements.

We consider these events to constitute a general event of default under the Allocation Agreement because over half of the borrower assurances for the loans reviewed had not been obtained. Under the Allocation Agreement signed by California, Treasury, in its sole discretion, may find a state to be in default of its Allocation Agreement if the state materially fails to comply with, meet or perform any term, covenant, agreement or other provision contained in the agreement. Further, Treasury may also find a state to be in default under the Allocation Agreement if any representation or certification made to Treasury is found to be inaccurate, false, incomplete, or misleading in any material respect. We believe California's September 2011 certification of compliance was materially inaccurate and false based on our audit findings. Additionally, because corrective actions to ensure that all borrower assurances have been obtained had not been implemented as of February 27, 2012, we believe California's December 2011 certification may also be materially inaccurate and false. Because we believe that California has triggered a general event of default under its Allocation Agreement, Treasury should consider whether future funding to California should be suspended or terminated.

To strengthen state accountability for compliance with SSBCI requirements, we made two prior recommendations, which Treasury subsequently implemented. In August 2011, we recommended that Treasury require borrowers and lenders to provide compliance assurances to designated state agencies responsible for administering the SSBCI funds, and require that participating states review them.[5] On March 6, 2012, Treasury issued *SSBCI National Standards for Compliance and Oversight*, which became effective on May 15, 2012. The standards state that Treasury expects participating states to establish a process to determine whether required borrower and lender certifications have been adequately documented. We believe that the standards, which were published in the Federal Register and e-mailed

---

[5] OIG-SBLF-11-002, STATE SMALL BUSINESS CREDIT INITATIVE: Treasury Needs to Strengthen State Accountability for Use of Funds, August 5, 2011.

to all participating states, adequately inform participants of their responsibility for collecting and reviewing borrower and lender assurances.

We also recommended that Treasury either modify the Allocation Agreement or amend its policy guidelines to require participating states to make representations that they are monitoring and enforcing compliance with Treasury guidelines and other program restrictions. Although Treasury initially declined to implement the recommendation, it has since issued national compliance standards for SSBCI that establish the oversight responsibilities of participating states and recommends a framework that states adopt for identifying, monitoring, and managing compliance risks. Therefore, we believe that Treasury has taken sufficient steps to strengthen state accountability for the use of SSBCI funds.

Recommendations

We recommend that the Deputy Assistant Secretary for Small Business, Housing and Community Development:

1. Recoup from the state of California the $133,250 in "recklessly" misused funds identified by the audit.

    Management Response

    Management stated that it will recoup from California the $133,250 in loan loss reserves identified as a misuse of funds.

    OIG Response

    OIG believes that Management's proposed action is responsive to the recommendation.

2. Require BTHA to provide documentation showing that its $153,777 in administrative expenses was based on actual costs. If BTHA is unable to do that, disallow the entire $153,777.

Management Response

Management stated that it has required California to provide supporting documentation for administrative expenses.

OIG Response

OIG believes that Management's proposed action is responsive to the recommendation.

3. Require CPCFA to provide documentation supporting the $7,211 in administrative expenses. If CPCFA is unable to do that, disallow the entire $7,211.

   #### Management Response

   Management stated that it has required California to provide supporting documentation for administrative expenses.

   #### OIG Response

   OIG believes that Management's proposed action is responsive to the recommendation.

4. Consider what, if any, additional action should be taken as a result of the inaccurate reporting of administrative expenses by CPCFA and BTHA.

   #### Management Response

   Management stated that in addition to recouping the misused funds from California, it will determine whether further action against the state is warranted.

   #### OIG Response

   OIG believes that Management's proposed action is responsive to the recommendation.

5. Require that California verify and report back the sex offender status of the borrower identified as residing with a registered sex offender, and identify who is using the loan proceeds.

Management Response

Management stated that it has required California to report back on the recommendation. California reported that it investigated and cleared the OIG's concern that a registered sex offender had the same residence as one of the borrowers. After investigation, California believes that neither of the borrowers associated with the loan are registered sex offenders or share an address with a registered sex offender.

OIG Response

OIG believes that Management's proposed action is responsive to the recommendation.

6. Require that California follow up with CPCFA and BTHA to ensure that all of the missing borrower and lender assurances identified by the audit are collected.

Management Response

Management stated that it has required California program officials to address missing borrower and lender certifications and assurances. Management noted that any loans still missing required assurances and certifications have been un-enrolled, and all other certification issues have been resolved.

OIG Response

OIG believes that Management's proposed action is responsive to the recommendation.

7. Determine whether there has been a general event of default under California's Allocation Agreement. If such an event has occurred, determine whether it warrants suspension or termination of future funding to the State.

Management Response

Management stated that in addition to recouping the misused funds from California, it will determine whether further action against the state is warranted.

OIG Response

OIG believes that Management's proposed action is responsive to the recommendation.

* * * * * *

We appreciate the courtesies and cooperation provided to our staff during the evaluation. If you wish to discuss the report, you may contact me at (202) 622-1090 or Lisa DeAngelis, Audit Director, at (202) 927-5621.

/s/
Debra Ritt
Special Deputy Inspector General for
Office of Small Business Lending Fund Program Oversight

Appendix 1
Objectives, Scope, and Methodology

The objectives of our audit were to: (1) test participant compliance with program requirements and prohibitions to identify reckless or intentional misuse; and (2) evaluate California's oversight of the California Capital Access Program (CalCAP) and the California Small Business Loan Guarantee Program (SBGLP) programs in order to assess the risk of waste, fraud, abuse, and non-compliance with the requirements of the Act. We also followed up on recommendations from our August 5, 2011 report[6] that Treasury (1) require each state to make a representation that it is aware of, monitoring and enforcing compliance with Treasury's policy guidelines and restrictions, and (2) require that the designated state agency responsible for administering SSBCI funds collect and review borrower and lender compliance assurances. California applied and was approved to receive $168.6 million through the State Small Business Credit Initiative (SSBCI). As of September 30, 2011, California had used approximately $3.6 million in Federal funds through its two participating programs, the CalCAP and the SBLGP.

The scope of our audit included all SSBCI small business loan enrollment activity in the SBLGP and CalCAP programs from the date of California's approval as an SSBCI participant, February 17, 2011, to the most recent quarterly reporting period, September 30, 2011. During this period, CalCAP had enrolled 449 loans, with a total loan enrollment of approximately $22 million. The total Federal contribution to the loan reserve funds associated with these loans is approximately $950,000. SBLGP had guaranteed 55 loans totaling approximately $9.9 million, utilizing approximately $2.47 million in SSBCI to guarantee these loans.

We interviewed the management and staff responsible for administering the SBLGP and CalCAP programs. These interviews were conducted in Sacramento, California, at the offices of the agencies responsible for administration of the programs. CalCAP is administered by the California Pollution Control Financing Authority (CPCFA). The California Business, Transportation, and Housing Agency (BTHA) serves as the overall administrator of the SBLGP. Interviews were conducted to understand and assess the following:

---

[6]OIG-SBLF-11-002, STATE SMALL BUSINESS CREDIT INITIATIVE: Treasury Needs to Strengthen State Accountability for Use of Funds, August 5, 2011.

Appendix 1
Objectives, Scope, and Methodology

- Administrative structures, including the capacity of BTHA and CPCFA to manage the increase in program activity from the influx of SSBCI funding.

- Procedures in place to process small business loans and ensure compliance with the requirements of the Act and associated Treasury guidelines.

- Accounting and reporting processes, including methodologies for calculating and reporting administrative expenses.

- Procedures for evaluating the financial and operational fitness of lenders participating in the programs.

In conjunction with interviews, we also reviewed associated policies, procedures, and other written guidance provided by SBLGP and CalCAP. In addition, we selected a sample of loans enrolled in SBLGP and CalCAP as of September 30, 2011, and performed testing to ensure all loans complied with the requirements and prohibitions of the Act and associated Treasury guidelines. We utilized a judgmental sampling methodology.

We selected 47 loans enrolled in CalCAP for our review. These 47 loans were originated by three different lending institutions throughout California. During the weeks ending November 4 and November 11, 2011, we conducted on-site reviews at each of the three lending institutions and compared the documentation in the loan files to the specific requirements and prohibitions of the Act and associated Treasury guidelines.

We selected 26 loans enrolled in SBLGP for review. The 26 loans were originated by 15 different lending institutions throughout California, and the loan guarantees were administered by six different Financial Development Corporations (FDC). During the weeks ending November 4, and November 11, 2011, we conducted on-site reviews of the loan files located at each of the six FDCs, and compared the documentation in the loan files to the specific requirements and prohibitions of the Act and associated Treasury guidelines.

We conducted our audit between October 2011 and March 2012 in accordance with Government Auditing Standards. Those standards

Appendix 1
Objectives, Scope, and Methodology

require that we plan and perform the audit to obtain sufficient, appropriate evidence to provide a reasonable basis for our findings and conclusions based on our audit objectives. We believe that the evidence obtained to address our audit objectives provides a reasonable basis for our findings and conclusions.

Appendix 2
Management Response

DEPARTMENT OF THE TREASURY
WASHINGTON, D.C. 20220

May 11, 2012

Debra Ritt
Special Deputy Inspector General for
  Office of Small Business Lending Fund Program Oversight
U.S. Department of the Treasury
1500 Pennsylvania Avenue, NW
Washington, DC 20220

Dear Ms. Ritt:

Thank you for the opportunity to review your draft report entitled *California's Use of Funds and Its Oversight of Programs Participating in the State Small Business Credit Initiative* (the Report). This letter provides the official response of the Department of the Treasury (Treasury).

We are pleased with the Report's finding that 96 percent of California's sampled State Small Business Credit Initiative (SSBCI) loans complied with program requirements. The Report demonstrates that the vast majority of SSBCI loans in California have been used as intended—to support new loans to eligible small businesses and to create jobs. Treasury also appreciates the Report's acknowledgement that the recently issued *SSBCI National Standards for Compliance and Oversight* will further strengthen state accountability and oversight of SSBCI funds. These enhancements will help make sure that SSBCI funding continues to facilitate small business growth as the program moves forward.

The Report does identify several instances of non-compliance with SSBCI program requirements. We take these issues very seriously and are committed to ensuring that SSBCI participants use taxpayer funds in an efficient and effective manner. Accordingly, on April 20, 2012, Treasury transmitted—with your consent—a draft copy of the Report to California and directed the state to submit a formal response addressing each item raised in the Report. California responded with the attached letter, which articulates in detail the measures California has implemented to address the Report's concerns. According to state officials, these actions include "a series of immediate and far-reaching steps to correct identified shortcomings, strengthen internal controls designed to prevent future non-compliance, and resolve issues associated with inadequate documentation of expenses, assurances and certifications."

More specifically, in response to your recommendations, Treasury required California program officials to address missing borrower and lender certifications and assurances. In its submission, California stated that it has obtained missing small business borrower and lender certifications and assurances for all sampled loans remaining in the program. Any loans still missing the required assurances and certifications have been un-enrolled, and all other certification issues related to sampled loans have been resolved (Recommendations 5 and 6). California intends to conclude a similar review of loans outside of the Report's sample by June 15, 2012. Treasury will monitor the state's progress and will track whether it has taken appropriate steps to address any outstanding certifications or assurances. California's letter

1

Appendix 2
Management Response

also describes a number of significant policy and internal control enhancements that the state has begun to implement to strengthen future oversight of Allocated Funds.

Also in response to your recommendations, Treasury required California to provide supporting documentation for administrative expenses (Recommendations 2 and 3). California submitted 289 pages of documentation. Treasury will review the material and will make a determination as to whether the expenses are permitted in accordance with the cost principals set forth in the Office of Management and Budget's Circular A-87 and the best practices recommended in the *SSBCI National Standards for Compliance and Oversight*. Treasury will only permit costs that are allowable, allocable, reasonable, and documented to be charged as administrative expenses.

Finally, Treasury will recoup from California the $133,250 in loan loss reserves identified as a misuse of funds (Recommendation 1). Treasury also will determine, after a full review of the policies, procedures, and data included in California's submission, whether further action against the state is warranted (Recommendations 4 and 7). Going forward, Treasury will monitor California's implementation of new policies and procedures intended to mitigate future deficiencies.

Thank you again for the opportunity to review the draft Report. We will continue to communicate with your office throughout this process. Treasury values the Report's contribution to SSBCI's long-term success, and we look forward to continued collaboration with your team.

Sincerely,

Don Graves, Jr.
Deputy Assistant Secretary for Small Business,
Community Development, and Affordable Housing
Policy

Attachment

Appendix 2
Management Response

STATE OF CALIFORNIA

EDMUND G. BROWN JR.
Governor

BRIAN P. KELLY
Acting Secretary

BILL LOCKYER
State Treasurer

BUSINESS, TRANSPORTATION AND HOUSING AGENCY

STATE TREASURER'S OFFICE

May 4, 2012

VIA ELECTRONIC MAIL

Mr. Don Graves, Jr.
Deputy Assistant Secretary for Small Business,
 Community Development and Housing Policy
United States Department of the Treasury
1500 Pennsylvania Avenue, NW
Room 2313
Washington, DC 20220

Dear Mr. Graves:

Thank you for giving the California Pollution Control Financing Authority (CPCFA) and the Business, Transportation and Housing Agency (BTHA) an opportunity to provide the State of California's (California) response to your letter dated April 20, 2012, surrounding the findings made by the United States Department of the Treasury (U.S. Treasury) Office of the Inspector General (OIG) in its draft report entitled "*California's Use of Funds and Its Oversight of Programs Participating in the State Small Business Credit Initiative*" (Report).

Overall, CPCFA and BTHA are pleased with the OIG's determination that "[a]pproximately 70, or 96 percent, of the 73 loans sampled complied with the requirements established for the [State Small Business Credit Initiative (SSBCI) program]." Although the SSBCI was a new program introduced and implemented rapidly, CPCFA and BTHA strove to understand and comply with federal requirements. During the seven-month period covered by the audit, approximately $3.6 million in SSBCI funds supported more than $33.2 million in eligible loans to meet the needs of small business and strengthen the economy, which is a critical objective of the SSBCI program. In fact, it should be noted that, during that same period, loans supported under the SSBCI program created or retained nearly 3,500 small business jobs.

Both CPCFA and BTHA worked diligently during the initial phase of the SSBCI program to continue existing strong controls over the California Capital Access Program (CalCAP) and Small Business Loan Guarantee Program (SBLGP), and to develop new protocols and controls to comply with emerging federal guidance related to the SSBCI program. Both entities acted in good faith to carefully gain an understanding of authorized uses of funds and documentation needed to support activities by reviewing the SSBCI Act, Allocation Agreement, initial SSBCI guidelines and revisions, and initial Frequently Asked Questions and updates. Importantly, we also had numerous discussions with the U.S. Treasury seeking additional guidance. CPCFA

BUSINESS, TRANSPORTATION AND HOUSING AGENCY • 980 9th Street, Suite 2450 • Sacramento CA 95814-2719 • (916) 323-5400
STATE TREASURER'S OFFICE • 915 Capitol Mall, C-15 • Sacramento, CA 95814 • (916) 653-2995
www.bth.ca.gov • www.treasurer.ca.gov • FLEX YOUR POWER! • BE ENERGY EFFICIENT!

Appendix 2
Management Response

Mr. Don Graves, Jr.
May 4, 2012
Page 2

and BTHA recognize the areas of non-compliance raised by the OIG audit and appreciate the opportunity to address and correct each of these areas. However, CFCPA and BTHA did not intentionally or recklessly misuse SSBCI funds; rather, both entities conscientiously followed and continue to comply with the federal provisions to the best of their ability given the uniqueness of the program. Thus, CPCFA and BTHA strongly believe that California should not be considered in default under the Allocation Agreement.

At the same time, both CPCFA and BTHA are committed to addressing the OIG's identified instances of non-compliance, including questioned costs of $160,988 (4.5 percent) and recommendations for the recoupment of $133,250 (3.7 percent) of the $3.6 million spent or obligated by California. Further, CPCFA and BTHA have also focused on the OIG's concerns raised about missing assurances and certifications. As noted in the sections that follow in response to the specific deficiencies delineated in your letter, CPCFA and BTHA have instituted a series of immediate and far-reaching steps to correct identified shortcomings, strengthen internal controls designed to prevent future non-compliance, and resolve issues associated with inadequate documentation of expenses, assurances and certifications.

Moreover, BTHA has investigated and cleared OIG's concern "that a registered sex offender had the same residence as one of the borrowers who had not provided an assurance as to his sex offender status." Only on April 20, 2012, was BTHA made aware of this allegation, and it immediately conducted additional research. Upon searching the California Department of Justice's Megan's Law website, which lists designated registered sex offenders in California, BTHA determined that neither of the two borrowers associated with the loan were classified as sex offenders, and no sex offender was listed as a resident at either of the two borrowers' residences or at the address of the place of business associated with the loan. BTHA did discover, however, that a sex offender was listed as having a last known address at a location with the exact same address number as the aforementioned place of business – but, the address was for a different street located within a tenth of a mile from the place of business. To ensure due diligence was fully exercised in this matter, BTHA requested the California Highway Patrol (CHP) to employ additional investigative steps. CHP indicated, however, that, absent a specific concern warranting a criminal background check, law enforcement also was limited to searching the Megan's Law website. In doing so, CHP verified BTHA's findings; thus, BTHA is confident that no loans were made to borrowers with convicted sex offender status and no further action is warranted at this time. Nevertheless, BTHA has implemented a new procedure to ensure sex offender status assurances are maintained on file at the agency.

Following are CPCFA's and BTHA's responses to address the specific deficiencies noted in your letter:

1. *Lack of documentation in accordance with the cost principles set forth in the Office of Management and Budget's (OMB's) Circular A-87 showing that administrative expenses claimed by the [BTHA] and the [CPCFA] were based on actual costs.*

    CPCFA Response:
    As part of its audit, the OIG determined that $17,230 charged for CPCFA's CalCAP administrative costs were reasonable, but that $7,211 of the $17,230 was not allowable or allocable because costs were not adequately supported by proper documentation of actual expenses. While CPCFA acknowledges the OIG finding, it is important to note that the $7,211 of administrative costs represents a small portion of the total actual costs that were allocable to SSBCI incurred by CPCFA during the audit reporting period but that were not yet charged or reimbursed to the program.

Appendix 2
Management Response

Mr. Don Graves, Jr.
May 4, 2012
Page 3

To support administrative costs, CPCFA used the following documents, which were provided to the OIG along with descriptions of the items used to comply with SSBCI and OMB Circular A-87 requirements:

- Reports from California's statewide financial accounting and reporting system (CALSTARS).
- Breakdown of the percentage of time each staff member was charging to the SSBCI funds.
- Descriptions of the methodologies employed for determining after-the-fact assignments of employee costs.
- Signed employee timesheets.
- Copies of the Interagency Agreement with the State Treasurer's Office (STO) to provide services to CPCFA in areas such as information technology, personnel, accounting, legal services, rent, and other indirect charges.

However, CPCFA now understands that support documentation for its personnel costs must also include a signed Personnel Activity Report reflecting an after-the-fact distribution of the actual activity for each employee on a monthly basis along with the other documentation already provided by CPCFA of actual personnel costs, signed time sheets, and a breakdown of percentage of time worked on the SSBCI Program to fully comply with provisions of OMB Circular A-87.

CPCFA has implemented a monthly Personnel Activity Report reflecting after-the-fact actual activity for each staff member charging costs to the SSBCI Program. The monthly Personnel Activity Report is supported by employee knowledge and certification, activity reports on loan and claim activities, time spent on various projects for the SSBCI Program, and any travel and training time that is allowable. These reports, signed by both the employee and his/her supervisor, are currently available for the March 2011 to June 2011 period under audit, as well as for subsequent periods as part of CPCFA's strengthened controls and practices, which are in addition to the existing CALSTARS fiscal reports reflecting the actual personnel costs for each staff member. (Supplemental documents are being provided under separate cover, but CPCFA Attachment 1 provides an example.) Going forward, CPCFA will support its administrative costs with an after-the-fact distribution of actual activity for each employee as documented on a signed Personnel Activity Report, along with fiscal CalSTARS reports and signed timesheets. Moreover, CPCFA will work closely with the STO accounting office and our contracted external consulting firm led by the former California State Auditor to improve processes and practices to ensure that direct and indirect administrative costs charged to the SSBCI program comply with applicable SSBCI and OMB requirements.

Unfortunately, one of CPCFA's staff is currently on an extended medical leave and is unavailable to sign the Personnel Activity Reports for the months between March 2011 and June 2011. The employee only worked on the SSBCI program for 25 percent of her time in March 2011, and devoted 100 percent of her time to the program during the April 2011 to June 2011 period. In accordance with OMB Circular A-87, if an employee works solely on a single Federal award or cost objective, either the employee or supervisory official having firsthand knowledge of the work performed by the employee may sign the Personnel Activity Report. Therefore, the personnel costs associated with this position for the month of March 2011 totaling $1,419.27 will be backed out since we do not have a signed activity report, while an updated Personnel Activity Report, signed by this employee's supervisor, for the April to June 2011 period will be submitted.

Appendix 2
Management Response

Mr. Don Graves, Jr.
May 4, 2012
Page 4

As mentioned earlier in this response section, CPCFA incurred more administrative costs than were charged/reimbursed under the SSBCI program. CPCFA reported and was reimbursed for $17,230 in allocable costs for the March 2011 to June 2011 time period. CPCFA submitted documentation showing $122,312 in eligible administrative costs. As a result of OIG's findings and CPCFA's additional analysis, we now recognize the following amounts should be removed from that figure: (a) $1,419.27 in personnel costs described above, (b) $21,390.08 of costs associated with its STO Interagency Agreement until further analysis and documentation can be reviewed and clarified, and (c) $9,902.84 in "Pro-Rata" costs, as these central service agency expenses must be charged to the federal program using a different mechanism - - for a total amount of $32,712.19 to be backed out, thus leaving $89,600.23 in total claimed expenses for the time period. (Supplemental documents are being provided under separate cover.) While much of the incurred costs for the time period have not been charged to the SSBCI program, CPCFA intends to report and seek reimbursement for allowable costs in the future using the appropriate method.

CPCFA has adjusted the overall total of allowable administrative charges that are eligible to be reported and reimbursed under the federal SSBCI program by $32,712.19, for a total amount of $89,600.23 as shown below:

- Personnel: $ 79,009.58
- Consultant: $ 7,109.00
- Mailing: $ 245.85
- Printing: $ 1,358.50
- Travel: $ 1,535.55
- Miscellaneous: $ 341.75
- Total Allowable Administrative Costs Eligible: $ 89,600.23

BTHA Response:
As noted in the OIG report, the SSBCI program does allow up to 5 percent of the initial tranche of funding to be used for administrative support, and the SBLGP came in under that threshold with administrative expenses of only 4.5 percent. The OIG report states that these expenses were reasonable, but not allowable or allocable because they were not adequately supported by actual expenses incurred or with proper documentation to validate the costs claimed.

The SBLGP is administered primarily by eleven Financial Development Corporations (FDC) located throughout the state. It should be noted that all of the $153,777 in administrative expenses were claimed by only seven of the eleven FDCs. Further, there were no expenses claimed for State staff time or other State program costs. While we do agree that these costs are reasonable, we now have an understanding as to why they may have been viewed as lacking proper documentation. Until recently, several FDCs did not track actual time worked on a daily basis on the SSBCI program as compared to other programs within their operations. Rather, some FDCs estimated how much time each employee spent on the program on a monthly basis and used that as the basis for their calculation. Others tracked it by actual hours worked, but did not have signed copies of timesheets. In no instance was the calculation of allowable SSBCI expenses less than what the FDCs charged the SSBCI program. In each case, the calculation of allowable expenditures exceeded, oftentimes to a great degree, the amount claimed.

Appendix 2
Management Response

Mr. Don Graves, Jr.
May 4, 2012
Page 5

Each FDC that claimed expenditures during the period of the audit has provided timesheets showing <u>actual</u> hours worked on the SSBCI program for those periods in which they claimed costs. In all cases, the FDCs have documented and justifiable costs exceeding the amounts claimed. These documents are being provided under separate cover, and we respectfully request that the full $153,777 in administrative expenses be allowed. The FDCs will submit copies of timesheets signed by each employee on the SSBCI program and his/her supervisor. Further, FDCs will submit payroll reports showing actual salaries and wages paid to all employees supporting the SSBCI program. The FDCs are also preparing and providing this detail to justify and document their expenses covering the period of time since the audit to the present (October 2011 – April 2012); this information will be available for review by the U.S. Treasury and the OIG. Any claims submitted for SSBCI expenses for State expenditures will be supported by Personnel Activity Reports, as required by OMB Circular A-87.

Additionally, BTHA is redirecting staff resources to assist in the monthly review of invoices received from the FDCs. Detailed procedures on what constitutes allowable costs have been developed and will be followed in each review. There will be two levels of review conducted before an invoice is approved and before the quarterly report to the U.S. Treasury is signed. A thorough review of all claims made from the inception of the program up to now will also be completed by the redirected staff. Detailed documentation that is clear, concise, and easily traceable will be available for any internal or external review. This process already has begun and will be completed by May 31, 2012.

2. *Missing lender certifications and assurances for loans identified by the Report.*

   CPCFA Response:
   Based on the OIG finding of missing lender assurances for the CalCAP loans they reviewed, CPCFA has taken immediate action to institute stronger controls to verify that required assurances are obtained and maintained in the State level CPCFA files, in addition to lender files.

   Specifically, as discussed in greater depth in the next section below, CPCFA has instituted new controls and practices that require lenders to submit all required written assurances to CPCFA for review and assessment **before** any funds will be disbursed. Further, the CPCFA Compliance Officer will review enrolled loans on a monthly basis to check whether required assurances were obtained and the loans complied with other applicable federal requirements. Moreover, on a regular and consistent basis, CPCFA will conduct on-site reviews of lender files to test compliance and correct any errors noted.

   BTHA Response:
   With one exception, copies of all of the missing lender certifications and assurances are being provided under separate cover. The loan that continues to be missing a lender certification has been determined to be non-compliant with the SSBCI program (due to lack of certification) and has been removed from the program. Another of the loans identified by the OIG as missing a lender certification, but for which such certification is included among the documents provided under separate cover, has also been removed from the program as it was one of the two loans identified in the OIG report as being guaranteed at 90 percent.

   The SBLGP is now obtaining from all FDCs copies of every lender certification and assurance for each loan guarantee currently enrolled in the program. If any SSBCI loan guarantee is missing certifications as of May 31, 2012, it will be removed from the SSBCI program. The SBLGP has also put in place a

Appendix 2
Management Response

Mr. Don Graves, Jr.
May 4, 2012
Page 6

procedure to obtain copies of all lender certifications from the FDCs **before** loan guarantees can be finalized. The SBLGP staff reviews the certifications and assurances to ensure that they meet all of the necessary requirements and, once the staff determines that they do, will notify the FDCs that they can proceed with executing the loan guarantee documents. The SBLGP will retain copies of all lender certifications and assurances and will have them available for review for any internal or external audit.

Finally, BTHA will redirect resources to ensure that each FDC is audited on-site once every year. BTHA is also actively recruiting to hire a new full-time Program Manager for the SBLGP who will oversee this responsibility. The on-site audit will focus on compliance with all SSBCI and State SBLGP requirements, and BTHA has an Audits and Performance Improvement unit within its organizational structure that will provide guidance and oversight for the audit of the FDCs.

3. *Missing borrower certifications and assurances for loans identified by the Report.*

   CPCFA Response:
   The OIG identified 30 loans with missing borrower assurances and one additional loan missing both the borrower assurances and a certification. Once we were provided a list of the loans on April 24, 2012, we reviewed the loans in question and determined that the primary issue was not whether borrower assurances were obtained, but rather whether the lender-obtained borrower assurances were adequate. What CPCFA found was that, of the 31 loans, 28 loans had borrower assurances, but in a format different than what OIG determined is required. The three remaining loans did not have the required assurances, with one of those missing both borrower and lender certifications.

   Based on the first U.S. Treasury guideline issued December 29, 2010, CPCFA staff interpreted the requirement for lenders to obtain borrower assurances to allow lenders to sign a certification assuring they obtained the following from each borrower on each loan enrolled in the program:

   - The loan is used for business purposes allowed by the U.S. Treasury.
   - The loan will not be used for purposes prohibited by the U.S. Treasury.
   - The loan will not be used to finance ineligible businesses prohibited by the U.S. Treasury.

   CPCFA staff added this wording to the certification section of the loan enrollment form in which each certification is initialed and the entire document is signed by an authorized representative of the financial institution based on the belief that the assurances could be reasonably obtained within the normal communication and activities between a lender and a borrower in the loan application process, without requiring the borrower to make the assurances specifically in writing. (CPCFA Attachment 2 provides a lender's letter of explanation regarding borrower assurances.)

   On May 2, 2011, when the new U.S. Treasury guidelines were announced, and from engaging in additional conversations with U.S. Treasury Representatives, CPCFA understood that the preference was for written borrower assurances, but that there was some discretion for the State to obtain the assurances in other ways. On May 11, 2011, U.S. Treasury released a revised Frequently Asked Questions document with a sample borrower assurance form that also included a clear statement that the form was not intended to replace other internal controls or protocols of a state's program and was to be used at the discretion of the state. Because CPCFA had a control system in place with lenders obtaining assurances in the required areas, and because no federal mandate or deadline had been placed on using

Appendix 2
Management Response

Mr. Don Graves, Jr.
May 4, 2012
Page 7

the sample forms provided, CPCFA continued the existing practices CPCFA had in place since April 1, 2011.

However, wanting to be fully compliant, staff also prepared written materials and scheduled conference-call training sessions to inform lenders about the use of the new documents with the revised assurances and certifications. Similar to other training sessions conducted with lenders on an as-needed basis over the years, CPCFA also held Lender Roundtable Conference calls with lenders during this time to discuss program changes and convey additional information needs. After each Lender Roundtable Conference call, all meeting notes and updated documents were emailed to lenders for reference and review, and were posted to the CPCFA website. Not realizing the new guideline was to be effective immediately and retroactive to April 1, 2011, CPCFA set an effective date for implementation of the new process of May 17, 2011.

While CPCFA quickly implemented the May 2, 2011 guidance for future loans, the initial borrower assurances and related lender certifications for the loans indicated in the OIG report were not to the satisfaction of the auditors. Thus, CPCFA has removed the loans in question from the federally funded CalCAP program and returned the premium contribution from these loans to the SSBCI CalCAP Federal Fund account. Additionally, in regard to the one CalCAP lender identified by the OIG as not obtaining any borrower assurances or certifications on CalCAP loans, CPCFA immediately suspended the lender from the program and disenrolled all effected loans after confirmation with lender staff. (Supplemental documents are being provided under separate cover.) Not only were the federal contributions returned to the SSBCI CalCAP Federal Fund account, but the lender will be required to undergo a thorough inspection of all files and receive extensive training before CPCFA will consider allowing it to participate in the program. Further, CPCFA is retroactively requiring all lenders to submit their borrower certifications to CPCFA for review on the additional 57 loans made during that audit time period prior to May 17, 2011. Any loan without compliant borrower certification and assurances will also be disenrolled from the federal-funded CalCAP program by June 15, 2012.

Moreover, CPCFA has completed the first on-site lender visit to review lender processes and documents for federal compliance as a part of an ongoing monitoring program through site visits and desk audits. In addition, CPCFA now requires lenders to submit all compliance certifications with the request for loan enrollment so that CPCFA analysts can ensure all documents are complete and compliant prior to enrolling loans in the program supported by federal funds.

CPCFA has operated in good faith to assess, review, interpret, and implement applicable federal requirements as part of the CalCAP, and has strived for compliance. The vast majority of our lenders obtained borrower assurances in a manner we believed were appropriate and compliant based on our knowledge and understanding of guidance received from U.S. Treasury and with the statutory requirements at the time. With one exception, all of the loans identified by OIG as non-compliant were enrolled during the first few weeks of program implementation, from April 1, 2011, to May 17, 2011. Since May 17, 2011, lenders have been instructed to obtain assurances in writing and OIG only found one non-compliant loan for the period from May 17, 2011, to September 30, 2011.

In summary, CPCFA understands the issues highlighted by the OIG and has taken the following steps:

Appendix 2
Management Response

Mr. Don Graves, Jr.
May 4, 2012
Page 8

In summary, CPCFA understands the issues highlighted by the OIG and has taken the following steps:
- Initiated a top-to-bottom review of every loan from the time period in question (April 1, 2011, to May 17, 2011) with the objective of removing any loan identified as missing written borrower certifications and assurances from the SSBCI program.
- Removed SSBCI funds for the identified loans from the loan loss reserve accounts and returned those funds to the SSBCI CalCAP Federal Fund account for use in other federally-eligible loans.
- Suspended one lender from participation in CalCAP.
- Instituted several new controls to ensure that all assurances and certifications are collected before loans are enrolled and SSBCI funds are transferred to loss reserve accounts. These controls include requiring copies of every signed assurance **before** disbursing federal funds, conducting regular on-site visits to review lender compliance, providing needed lender training, and having CPCFA's Compliance Officer review, monthly, documents on file.

BTHA Response:
As with the lender certifications, BTHA acknowledges that there were missing borrower certifications. With one exception – the same 90-percent guarantee that was missing the lender certification – copies of all of the missing borrower certifications have been obtained and are included for reference under separate cover. The same measures that are being taken to improve the process to ensure that all lender certifications and assurances are obtained **before** loan guarantees are finalized, apply to borrower certifications. BTHA will ensure that no loan currently enrolled in the program lacks a borrower certification and, by May 31, 2012, will disenroll from the SSBCI program any guarantee that lacks one. Additionally, the SBLGP has implemented the same review practices for borrower certifications and assurances as has been outlined above for lender certifications and assurances.

4. *Lack of adequate controls to ensure that certifications and representations made by California to [U.S.] Treasury as part of the quarterly or annual reports were accurate and based on a good faith examination of compliance with applicable laws, agreements and guidance.*

CPCFA Response:
For the time period of the audit, CPCFA believed it was in compliance with applicable laws, agreements and guidance. Further, CPCFA believes that it acted in good faith in attempting to apply SSBCI requirements in the areas identified by OIG.

Although controls were in place over lender and loan enrollment, claims processing, and bank reconciliations, the OIG identified two primary control deficiencies in the CalCAP program: missing assurances/certifications and inadequate documentation of personnel expenses. CPCFA acknowledges the items raised by the OIG and is appreciative for the opportunity to better understand the intricacies of the SSBCI program and related guiding circulars issued by the Federal Office of Management and Budget. CPCFA has strengthened controls in general, in addition to tightening controls specific to the OIG issue areas, to better ensure that certifications and representations are fully accurate and comply with applicable laws, agreements, and guidance.

Loan database records are now reconciled with bank statements and loan source documents.

Appendix 2
Management Response

Mr. Don Graves, Jr.
May 4, 2012
Page 9

To further elaborate on the good-faith efforts of CPCFA related to the issues raised by OIG:

1. **Borrower assurances/certifications**: CPCFA lenders certified that they had the necessary certifications and assurances on every loan, including those identified by OIG. In fact, lenders verified they had obtained borrower assurances on all but three (3) loans identified by OIG. Based on written guidance provided by U.S. Treasury in early 2011, CPCFA initially believed it had some level of discretion regarding the application of borrower assurance requirements. (CPCFA Attachment 3 provides a chart comparing assurance requirements with CPCFA actions.) As such, CPCFA allowed lenders to obtain assurances in any manner they chose as long as it included all required assurances and the lender certified to CPCFA that they had received the assurances. When U.S. Treasury guidelines were revised on May 2, 2011, CPCFA recognized that the level of specificity in the guidelines was best met with written assurances. CPCFA immediately started the process to change its regulations and provide new training to lenders on this issue. Instantaneous adoption was not practical given the CalCAP regulation process in place in California. However, these guidelines were changed and implemented on May 17, 2011.

    For the time period April 1, 2011, to May 17, 2011, CPCFA believed it had a compliant process for obtaining assurances and related certifications from lenders. Once it was recognized that assurances should be in writing, CPCFA instituted new requirements and controls effective May 17, 2011. CPCFA performed a line-by-line, detailed comparison of its CalCAP forms with federal requirements each time U.S. Treasury issued new guidance documents, and these reviews have resulted in new forms and documents to be used by lenders. Moreover, an additional control has been implemented for lenders to submit borrower assurances to CPCFA for review and documentation **before** any loan is enrolled using SSBCI funds. (CPCFA Attachment 4 demonstrates CPCFA communications with lenders regarding SSBCI program compliance.)

2. **Personnel Expenses**: CPCFA has documentation associated with personnel expenses. For instance, at the time of submitting the annual and quarterly reports, CPCFA had signed timesheets for every employee working on the SSBCI program, after-the-fact activity reports for every employee, and payroll records supporting salary and benefit costs. Upon further examination, CPCFA now realizes that each employee and their supervisor should have signed their Personnel Activity Reports in addition to their timesheets. Thus, CPCFA has now obtained the required employee/supervisor time certification for the months under audit and subsequent months through March 2012. Moreover, CPCFA has implemented a new control protocol for all timesheets and signed Personnel Activity Reports to be gathered and reviewed for accuracy by the CPCFA's Compliance Officer on a monthly basis.

    It is important to note that, at the time of signing the certifications and representations in the quarterly and annual report, CPCFA staff acted in good faith and believed that data reported was accurate and that program activities and costs were in compliance with applicable laws, agreements, and guidance. CPCFA had systems in place to verify and validate the numerical information provided, for lenders to certify their compliance with program requirements, and to perform certain compliance monitoring protocols. CPCFA is confident that these systems, combined with the newly strengthened controls put in place, will be adequate and will better ensure compliance with applicable federal regulations.

Appendix 2
Management Response

Mr. Don Graves, Jr.
May 4, 2012
Page 10

BTHA Response:
We appreciate learning of areas where we have fallen short in complying with certain aspects of the SSBCI program and have taken steps to address each of these areas. We will continue to identify additional areas of improvement as we move forward with this program. We take all of the findings and recommendations of the OIG report seriously and we are confident that the measures we have outlined in this response will strengthen compliance with all program requirements. We believe that previous certifications were made in good faith and were based on the best efforts and intentions of SBLGP staff at that time.

As previously noted, BTHA is redirecting staff resources to oversee the review of monthly submissions of expenses from the FDCs and the preparation of the quarterly/annual SSBCI report. Detailed procedures have been developed on the expense review and report preparation and will be strictly followed. The focus of this review is to ensure that all expenses are properly justified and documented and that all loans enrolled in the program meet SSBCI requirements. There will be two levels of review for each of these processes (monthly expenses and quarterly/annual reports) before the expenses are approved or the reports are signed.

We also recognize the importance of ensuring that each FDC completely and fully understands all aspects of the SSBCI program and that the program be implemented consistently by all eleven FDCs. Although training sessions have been conducted to explain and outline the aspects of the SSBCI program, it is evident that more work needs to be done. Consequently, we have scheduled monthly conference calls with all FDCs and the SBLGP staff to review each section of the Allocation Agreement and Annexes. These conference calls will be held on the second Tuesday of each month and will remain calendared through the life of the SSBCI program. Ensuring that each FDC understands the policies and guidelines of the program is an important step in ensuring that they comply.

Additionally, the SBLGP holds a quarterly in-person meeting with all of the FDCs. A phone conference call with the Relationship Manager and Compliance Manager from the U.S. Treasury SSBCI program will be included as an ongoing agenda item at each quarterly meeting. As part of the most recent quarterly meeting, held on April 24, 2012, a conference call was held with the Relationship Manager and Compliance Manager to discuss specific aspects of the SSBCI guidelines. Just as we found this discussion to be very helpful, we expect future discussions will be beneficial in that each FDC will hear the same, consistent interpretation and conversation on the various guidelines outlining the program. As policies and procedures change regularly, it is important that we respond and react in an appropriate manner.

Finally, BTHA will redirect resources to ensure that each FDC is audited on-site once every year. BTHA is also actively recruiting to hire a new full-time Program Manager for the SBLGP who will oversee this responsibility. The on-site audit will focus on compliance with all SSBCI and State SBLGP requirements, and BTHA has an Audits and Performance Improvement unit within its organizational structure that will provide guidance and oversight for the audit of the FDCs.

Appendix 2
Management Response

Mr. Don Graves, Jr.
May 4, 2012
Page 11

5. *Lack of adequate controls to ensure all Allocated Funds were used for authorized purposes as described in Section 4.2 of the Allocation Agreement.*

CPCFA Response:
To ensure that allocated funds are used for authorized purposes, CPCFA regularly employs a number of procedures to ensure the accuracy and compliance of program activity. Moreover, CPCFA staff diligently reviewed the cost principles outlined in OMB Circular A-87 and gathered supporting documentation of personnel costs in good faith. There was no willful intent to evade the requirements; rather, based on staff interpretation, CPCFA believed its documentation requirements and control procedures were in compliance.

As it relates to the OIG's finding of $7,211 in questioned personnel costs lacking sufficient supporting documentation, the OIG did not identify for CPCFA the specific nature or issues surrounding the questioned cost exceptions. However, CPCFA is confident that personnel costs charged and reimbursed against the SSBCI program were for authorized purposes and supported the objectives of the SSBCI program. Employees worked on activities that directly aligned with the federal program, such as lender and loan enrollment, claims processing, and lender training. To account for the time and effort spent on the SSBCI program, employees completed timesheets and staff prepared Personnel Activity Reports detailing percentage of time worked on SSBCI activities and methodologies for determining after-the-fact SSBCI fundable work. However, although CPCFA maintains signed timesheets for each employee, the Personnel Activity Reports did not have employee and supervisory signatures.

For the audit period in question, CPCFA has obtained employee/supervisor signatures on the Personnel Activity Reports. On a go-forward basis, CPCFA has developed and implemented new controls where its Compliance Officer now obtains and reviews all financial and program data on a monthly basis to identify underlying supporting documentation (such as financial records, invoices, and Personnel Activity Reports) and to ensure the nature of activities and costs are consistent with the SSBCI program requirements and authorized purposes.

CPCFA continues to revisit and reassess this process and related procedures for documentation; specifically CPCFA's Compliance Officer and senior management are participating in this review and working with an external consulting firm led by the former California State Auditor to better ensure that we are fully compliant. Moreover, our Compliance Officer will periodically test our system against currently available OMB and SSBCI requirements to ensure ongoing compliance.

Based on a recent assessment, CPCFA has documented $79,009.58 in allowable personnel costs for the time period under audit that are supported by signed timesheets, signed after-the-fact Personnel Activity Reports, and accurate payroll records. Thus, CPCFA has more reimbursable personnel costs than the initial $7,211 of questioned personnel costs. CPCFA intends to recover the allowable personnel costs in the future.

Further, CPCFA's recent assessment reveals that improved documentation is needed to support expenses associated with a contract with the STO for accounting and support services in addition to a share of State central service costs charged through "Pro-Rata." While the STO contract costs are not part of any funds that have been charged/reimbursed using SSBCI funds at this point, CPCFA will be working with the STO's accounting staff to ensure consistency with California cost allocation methodologies and

Appendix 2
Management Response

Mr. Don Graves, Jr.
May 4, 2012
Page 12

federal requirements related to allowability and documentation for claiming administrative expenses, and will be submitting reimbursement requests for appropriately allowable costs in the future.

BTHA Response:
We recognize the deficiency in documenting and justifying allowable and allocable administrative costs. The SBLGP did receive invoices from each FDC claiming SSBCI administrative costs and did require that the FDCs only claim actual costs. However, the methodology used needed to be changed to conform to OMB Circular A-87. We now have a better understanding of how to document these costs to demonstrate and ensure that the costs are properly documented, and we believe these new procedures will ensure full compliance with the federal guidelines. We appreciate and agree with the OIG report that the administrative costs were reasonable, as demonstrated by documentation that is provided under separate cover.

As previously stated, BTHA is redirecting staff resources to assist in the monthly review of invoices received from the FDCs. Detailed procedures on what constitutes allowable costs pursuant to OMB Circular A-87 have been drafted and will be followed in each review. There will be two levels of review conducted before an invoice is approved and before the quarterly report to the U.S. Treasury is signed. A thorough review of all claims made from the inception of the program up to now will also be completed by the redirected staff. Detailed documentation that is clear, concise, and easily traceable will be available for any internal or external review. This process has begun and will be completed by May 31, 2012.

We do not anticipate there to be any changes to the allocated funds/allowable costs section of any of the previously submitted quarterly reports or to the annual report as a result of this review. We are confident that all of the costs reported and claimed by the FDCs are well-supported and documentation has been gathered to justify these claims.

In addition, the FDCs now have a more clear understanding of what they must track each month and provide to the SBLGP staff to substantiate the amounts that they are claiming for SSBCI costs. No expenses will be approved by the SBLGP staff unless they meet the criteria that have been specified in the procedures.

Finally, BTHA will redirect resources to ensure that each FDC is audited on-site once every year. BTHA is also actively recruiting to hire a new full-time Program Manager for the SBLGP who will oversee this responsibility. The on-site audit will focus on compliance with all SSBCI and State SBLGP requirements, and BTHA has an Audits and Performance Improvement unit within its organizational structure that will provide guidance and oversight for the audit of the FDCs.

6. *Lack of adequate controls to ensure all Allocated Funds were used in accordance with the applicable restrictions included in Section 4.4 of the Allocation Agreement.*

CPCFA Response:
As part of the existing CalCAP program prior to April 2011, CPCFA had systems in place before the first loan was enrolled using SSBCI funds to carry out provisions outlined under the five components of Section 4.4 of the Allocation Agreement (a through e). These systems and processes ensure that only

Appendix 2
Management Response

Mr. Don Graves, Jr.
May 4, 2012
Page 13

qualified loans are enrolled, proper assurances are obtained, and funds are used in a proper manner through use of standard review checklists, file documentation review, and several levels of supervisory and managerial review conducted during a loan enrollment process and on an ongoing basis.

If there is any indication that funds are not properly being used, CPCFA will, and has, appropriately recovered funds as necessary. For example, in early 2011, CPCFA discovered that there was a rounding error involving less than two cents that affected more than 100 loans. Although these loans involved funding at a small fraction just slightly over 3.5 percent, immediately upon discovery of this issue, CPCFA instructed the trustee bank to reverse a specified number of cents per transaction and transfer the funds back into the SSBCI account.

Other CPCFA controls designed to ensure compliance of loans enrolled in the SSBCI program include the following:

- Developing and testing compliance procedures by a dedicated staff person.
- Training lenders in CalCAP procedures, especially those related to SSBCI.
- Conducting regular roundtable conference calls with lenders to review new and existing procedures and answer questions of the lenders.
- Making copies of all procedures available on the CPCFA website.
- Developing detailed lender enrollment forms, including verification from the lender that it will comply with required rules, regulations and procedures.
- Developing comprehensive loan enrollment forms, including certifications by lenders that they are complying with items associated with the use of SSBCI forms.
- Adopting key federal requirements into State regulation using the California regulation adoption process.
- Obtaining signed assurances from borrowers and maintaining them in CPCFA files for every enrolled loan.
- Performing a three-step review of every loan before funding is approved, including a (1) compliance assessment by an analyst, (2) review and approval by a manger, and (3) check and approval by the Executive Director or Deputy Executive Director.
- Conducting a post-funding review, by the Compliance Officer, of every loan enrollment.
- Performing monthly and quarterly reconciliations reviewing bank statements, invoices, lender and loan documentation, and using CPCFA automated program tracking systems to further verify and confirm the proper use and transfer of SSBCI funds.

Recognizing that there is always room to enhance and improve systems of controls, CPCFA has engaged an external consulting firm headed by the former California State Auditor to review and analyze our existing processes and procedures and produce an updated desk-reference manual outlining the framework for operating the SSBCI program and containing procedures used to ensure compliance with all applicable federal guidelines, provisions, and regulations. This desk manual will be fully consistent and compliant with the latest National Standards for Compliance and Oversight document.

Appendix 2
Management Response

Mr. Don Graves, Jr.
May 4, 2012
Page 14

BTHA Response:

As noted in the OIG report, the SBLGP did seek approval to move forward with two loan guarantees that had originally been negotiated at a 90-percent-guarantee rate at the time the 90-percent limit was authorized. We did not receive a denial of our request and to the best of our knowledge, we provided all of the information that U.S. Treasury requested in regards to the two loans in question. However, we now recognize that we should have had express approval to enroll these guarantees in the SSBCI program and, absent the affirmative approval of the U.S. Treasury as required in Section 4.4 (a) of the Allocation Agreement, we acknowledge these guarantees to be non-compliant with current SSBCI guidelines. We have since removed these guarantees from the SSBCI program. The SBLGP never intended to deliberately ignore the changes in policy guidelines or misuse any SSBCI funds. These two loans met all other criteria for the SBLGP and were made to legitimate and valid businesses for legitimate and valid business purposes.

We also recognize that one loan was guaranteed for a business purpose that did not meet the requirements of the SSBCI program. The loan in question has been disenrolled from the SSBCI program. The new controls and oversight efforts – principally the annual on-site audit of each FDC – will ensure that the FDCs are complying with all aspects of the SSBCI policies and guidelines, and that all guarantees are in accordance with the restrictions of the Allocation Agreement.

The SBLGP is being much more vigilant in responding to changes in policy to the SSBCI guidelines. With any future changes, we will implement all changes effective as of the date of the policy. Any loan guarantee approved on or after the date of implementation of a new or revised policy will adhere strictly to the policy in place at that time, regardless of where in the negotiation stage the loan processing may be.

The SBLGP will also ensure that each of the eleven FDCs is trained and understands completely any new or revised changes to SSBCI policy guidelines. In instances where clarity is needed on policy direction, the SBLGP will continue to seek clarification from the U.S. Treasury via conference call or email as to the intent and official interpretation by the U.S. Treasury of the stated guidelines. The two-level review process of information contained in all monthly and quarterly reporting from the FDCs will help ensure that the allocated funds are used in accordance with all restrictions included in the Allocation Agreement.

Finally, BTHA will redirect resources to ensure that each FDC is audited on-site once every year. BTHA is also actively recruiting to hire a new full-time Program Manager for the SBLGP who will oversee this responsibility. The on-site audit will focus on compliance with all SSBCI and State SBLGP requirements, and BTHA has an Audits and Performance Improvement unit within its organizational structure that will provide guidance and oversight for the audit of the FDCs. We are confident that this internal audit process that is now being implemented will help ensure that each FDC is adhering to the proper use of allocated funds. We believe it is important that SBLGP staff conduct on-site audits at the place of business of each FDC so that the auditors have access to all records and files held by the FDCs.

Appendix 2
Management Response

Mr. Don Graves, Jr.
May 4, 2012
Page 15

In summary, BTHA controls designed to ensure compliance of loans enrolled in the SSBCI program include the following:

- All FDCs have been instructed to track the actual number of hours worked by each employee on the SSBCI, State, and all other programs.
- Invoices submitted by FDCs are required to include copies of timesheets signed by the employee and supervisor. FDCs will also submit payroll reports showing actual salaries/wages paid to all employees.
- Claims submitted for SSBCI expenses for State expenditures will be supported by Personal Activity Reports.
- Detailed procedures on what constitutes allowable costs have been developed and will be followed in the monthly review of invoices.
- Invoices will be subjected to two levels of review before being approved, and before quarterly reports to the U.S. Treasury are signed.
- Staff resources have been redirected to assist with the monthly review of invoices.
- Procedures have been implemented requiring SBLGP staff to obtain, review and maintain a copy of each lender and borrower certification before loan guarantees are finalized.
- Staff resources are being redirected to ensure that each FDC is audited on-site once a year, focusing on compliance with all SSBCI and State SBLGP requirements.
- Guidance and oversight for the audit of the FDCs will be provided by BTHA's Audits and Performance Improvement unit.
- Detailed procedures for quarterly and annual reports have been developed and will be strictly followed.
- Two levels of review of quarterly and annual reports will be performed before approval.
- Enhanced communication and training with FDCs and SBLGP staff will be provided through monthly conference calls and quarterly in-person meetings.
- Quarterly in-person meetings with all FDCs are conducted and, beginning in April 2012, include a conference call with the U.S. Treasury.
- A full-time Program Manager for the SBLGP is being actively recruited to oversee the SSBCI Program.
- Clarifications of SSBCI policy guidelines, when necessary, will be requested from the U.S. Treasury.

As the responses in this letter demonstrate, CPCFA and BTHA take very seriously the OIG audit report. We have addressed all of the issues associated with missing paperwork for enrolled loans by either obtaining the paperwork or disenrolling the loans. CPCFA suspended a lender and removed their non-compliant loans from the program for failure to adhere to program requirements. We have documented all expenses identified as needing further documentation. We acknowledge the issues with non-compliant loans and have removed those loans from the program. We have instituted new controls, including on-site visits and audits of program participants, additional review mechanisms to ensure loans are compliant before enrollment, and new training and oversight of program participants.

For these reasons, we believe that further punitive steps involving the California programs are unnecessary.

Appendix 2
Management Response

Mr. Don Graves, Jr.
May 4, 2012
Page 16

Again, CPCFA and BTHA thank you for the opportunity to address the OIG items and to provide additional insight into our program controls. If you have questions or need additional information related to these responses, please do not hesitate to contact Michael Paparian by telephone at (916) 657-4921 or email at mpaparian@treasurer.ca.gov, as well as William Davidson by telephone at (916) 324-7519 or email at william.davidson@bth.ca.gov.

Sincerely,

William Davidson
Deputy Secretary, Administration and Finance
Business, Transportation and Housing Agency

Michael Paparian
Executive Director
California Pollution Control Financing Authority

Attachments

Appendix 3
Distribution List

Department of the Treasury
    Deputy Secretary
    Office of Strategic Planning and Performance Management
    Office of Accounting and Internal Control

Office of Management and Budget
    OIG Budget Examiner

United States Senate
    Chairman and Ranking Member
    Committee on Small Business and Entrepreneurship

    Chairman and Ranking Member
    Committee on Finance

    Chairman and Ranking Member
    Committee on Banking, Housing and Urban Affairs

United States House of Representatives
    Chairman and Ranking Member
    Committee on Small Business

    Chairman and Ranking Member
    Committee on Financial Services

Government Accountability Office
    Comptroller General of the United States

www.ingramcontent.com/pod-product-compliance
Lightning Source LLC
Chambersburg PA
CBHW081802170526
45167CB00008B/3292